PIANO FUN
CLASSICAL FAVORITES
FOR ADULT BEGINNERS
Arranged by Brenda Dillon

CONTENTS

Orchestrations by Peter Deneff

To access audio visit:
www.halleonard.com/mylibrary

Enter Code
4660-5126-4168-8444

T0039475

ISBN 978-1-5400-2468-8

HAL•LEONARD®

7777 W. Bluemound Rd. P.O. Box 13819 Milwaukee, WI 53213

Visit Hal Leonard Online at
www.halleonard.com

Contact Us:
Hal Leonard
7777 West Bluemound Road
Milwaukee, WI 53213
Email: info@halleonard.com

In Europe contact:
Hal Leonard Europe Limited
42 Wigmore Street
Marylebone, London, W1U 2RN
Email: info@halleonardeurope.com

In Australia contact:
Hal Leonard Australia Pty. Ltd.
4 Lentara Court
Cheltenham, Victoria, 3192 Australia
Email: info@halleonard.com.au

PERFORMANCE NOTES

Introduction

Welcome to *Piano Fun: Classical Favorites for Adult Beginners*, a collection of lead sheets and arrangements for the beginning pianist who has learned how to read music and wants to play easy arrangements of classical melodies.

About the Orchestrations

Every arrangement and lead sheet includes a play-along track filled with beautifully orchestrated arrangements by film composer and music producer Peter Deneff. To access the tracks, simply go to **www.halleonard.com/mylibrary** and enter the code found on page 1. This will grant you instant access to every file. You can download to your computer, tablet, or phone, or stream the audio live. You can also use our *PLAYBACK+* multi-functional audio player to slow down or speed up the tempo, change keys, or set loop points. This feature is available exclusively from Hal Leonard and is included with the price of this book!

Triad/Chords

- Triads are three-note chords, and seventh chords have four notes.

- Major triads built on the white piano keys can be divided into three sets:

C	E	G
F	A	C	All three pitches are white piano keys or W-W-W
G	B	D	

D	F♯	A
E	G♯	B	The middle pitch is a black key or W-B-W
A	C♯	E

| B | D♯ | F♯ | The middle pitch and top pitch are black keys or W-B-B |

- Major triads can be altered to become minor, diminished or augmented.

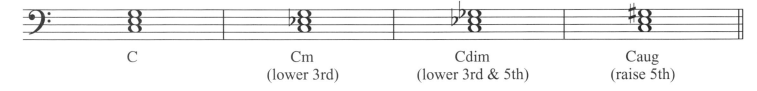

C   Cm (lower 3rd)   Cdim (lower 3rd & 5th)   Caug (raise 5th)

- Seventh chords are spelled with four notes. The bottom note is the root, the next note above is the 3rd, the note above the third is the 5th, and the top note is the 7th.

- Major 7th chords can be altered to become dominant 7th, minor 7th and diminished 7th.

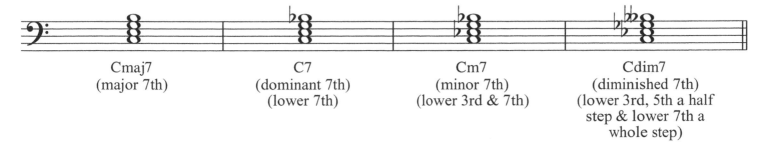

Cmaj7
(major 7th)

C7
(dominant 7th)
(lower 7th)

Cm7
(minor 7th)
(lower 3rd & 7th)

Cdim7
(diminished 7th)
(lower 3rd, 5th a half
step & lower 7th a
whole step)

Root or Close Position

Chords can be played in two positions—root or close position. Learning to play close position chords is helpful because the hand doesn't have to skip around as much. Also, chords sound best when they are played in the octave below middle C, and close position chords make this easier.

- When the name of the chord is on the bottom, it's called root position (CEG).
- When another pitch of the chord is on the bottom, it's called an inversion.
- Close position is found by moving to the nearest chord tones rather than having the hand move from root to root.

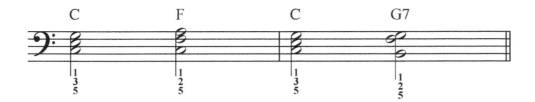

Learning Lead Sheets

- Lead sheets sound best when the LH (left hand) chords are played in the octave below middle C.
- Play the RH (right hand) melody an octave above where it's written.
- The chord symbols (alphabet letters) are written above the melody.
- Slow the tempo so moving from chord to chord is easier.
- The orchestration plays the melody, but it can also be sung or hummed by the students.

LEAD SHEETS

Canon in D

By Johann Pachelbel
Arranged by Brenda Dillon

Carmen Suite No. 1

(Intermezzo)

By Georges Bizet
Arranged by Brenda Dillon

Etude
Op. 10, No. 3

By Frédéric Chopin
Arranged by Brenda Dillon

Evening Prayer

from HANSEL AND GRETEL

Music by Engelbert Humperdinck
Words by Adelheid Wette
Arranged by Brenda Dillon

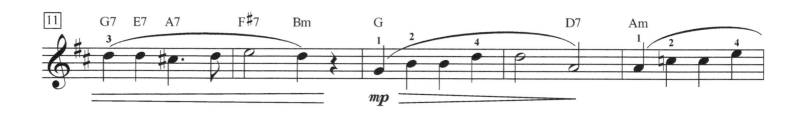

Für Elise, WoO 59

By Ludwig van Beethoven
Arranged by Brenda Dillon

Largo
from SYMPHONY NO. 9 ("NEW WORLD")

By Antonin Dvořák
Arranged by Brenda Dillon

Liebestraum
(Dream of Love)

By Franz Liszt
Arranged by Brenda Dillon

O mio babbino caro

from GIANNI SCHICCHI

By Giacomo Puccini
Arranged by Brenda Dillon

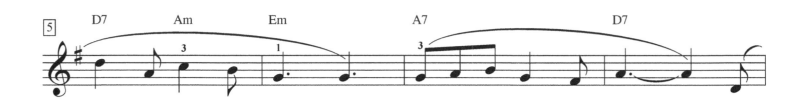

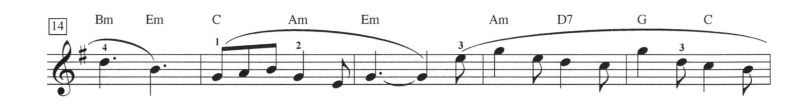

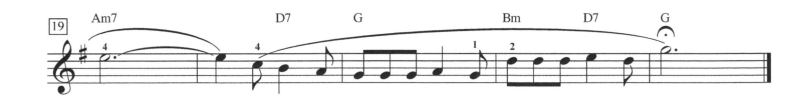

Polovetzian Dance No. 1
from PRINCE IGOR

By Alexander Borodin
Arranged by Brenda Dillon

Rhapsody on a Theme of Paganini
Variation XVIII

By Sergei Rachmaninoff
Arranged by Brenda Dillon

Sheep May Safely Graze

By Johann Sebastian Bach
Arranged by Brenda Dillon

Piano Sonata No. 14 in C# Minor

("Moonlight"), Op. 27, No. 2 First Movement Theme

By Ludwig van Beethoven
Arranged by Brenda Dillon

Swan Lake

By Pyotr Ilyich Tchaikovsky
Arranged by Brenda Dillon

To a Wild Rose

from WOODLAND SKETCHES, OP. 51, NO. 1

By Edward MacDowell
Arranged by Brenda Dillon

ARRANGEMENTS

Canon in D

By Johann Pachelbel
Arranged by Brenda Dillon

Carmen Suite No. 1

(Intermezzo)

By Georges Bizet
Arranged by Brenda Dillon

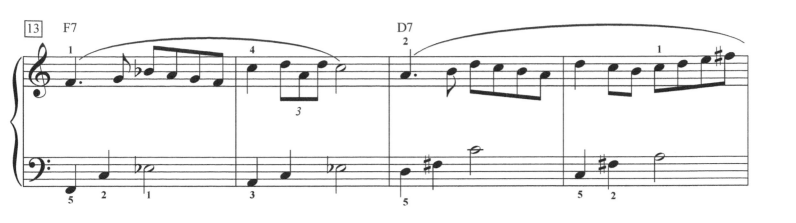

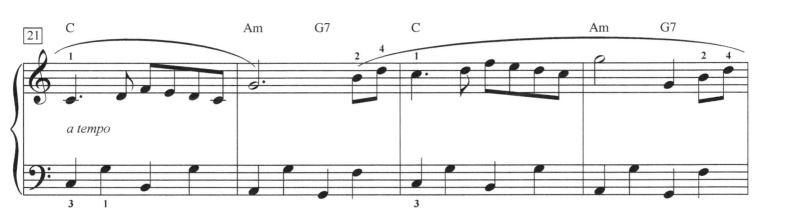

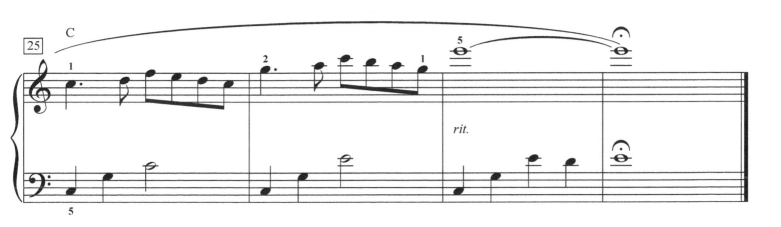

Etude
Op. 10, No. 3

By Frédéric Chopin
Arranged by Brenda Dillon

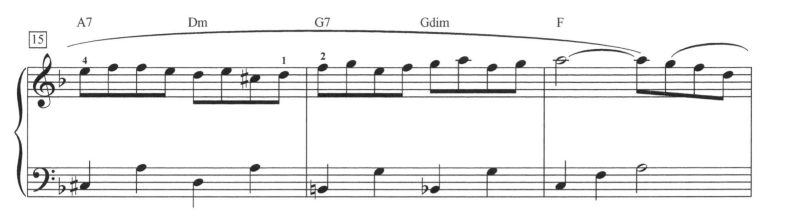

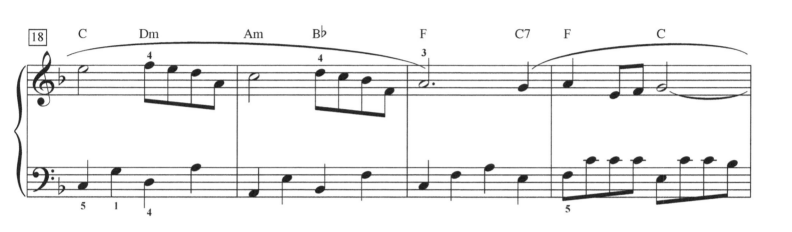

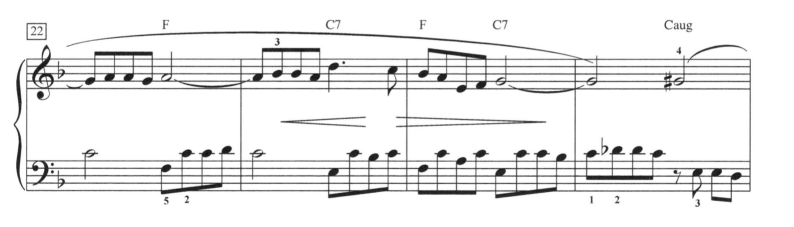

25

Evening Prayer
from HANSEL AND GRETEL

Music by Engelbert Humperdinck
Words by Adelheid Wette
Arranged by Brenda Dillon

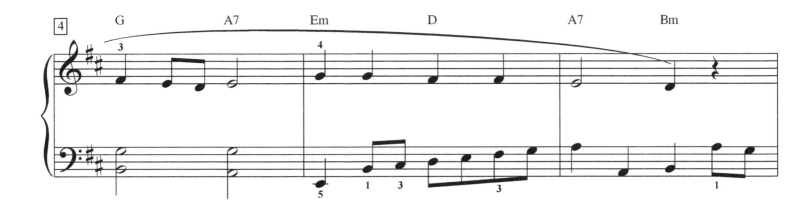

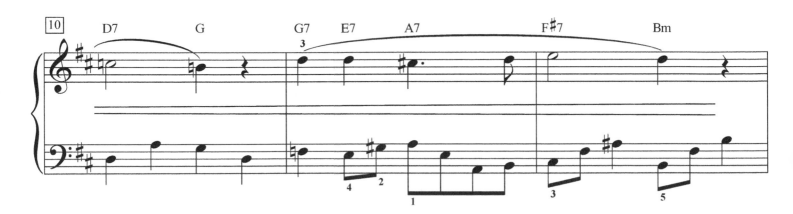

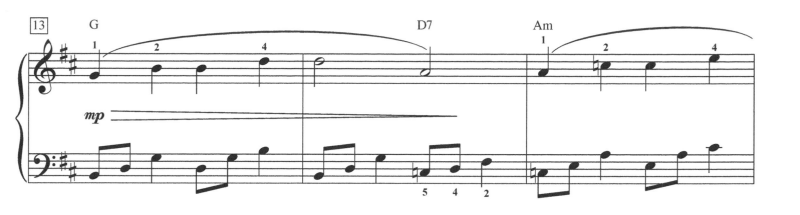

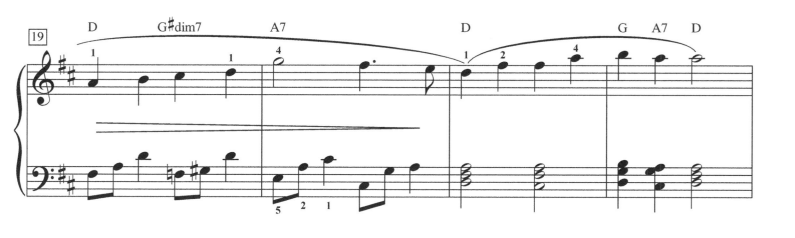

Für Elise, WoO 59

By Ludwig van Beethoven
Arranged by Brenda Dillon

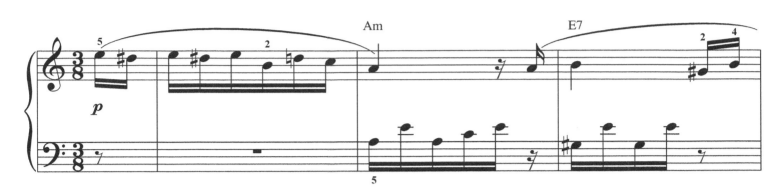

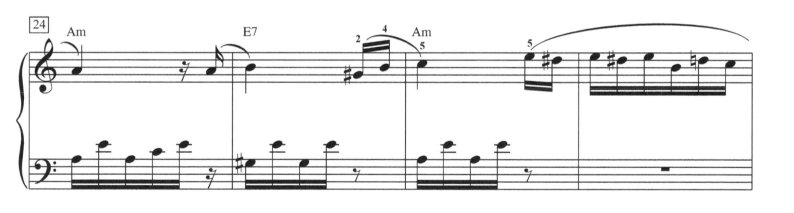

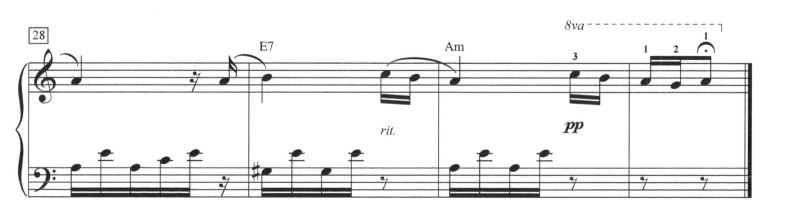

Largo
from SYMPHONY NO. 9 ("NEW WORLD")

By Antonin Dvořák
Arranged by Brenda Dillon

Liebestraum
(Dream of Love)

By Franz Liszt
Arranged by Brenda Dillon

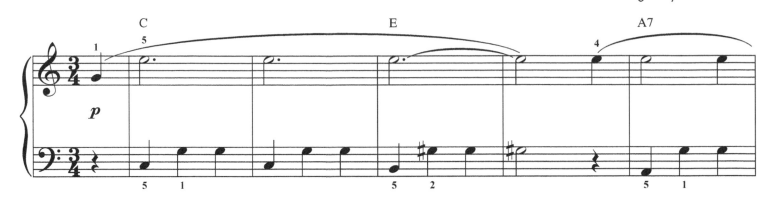

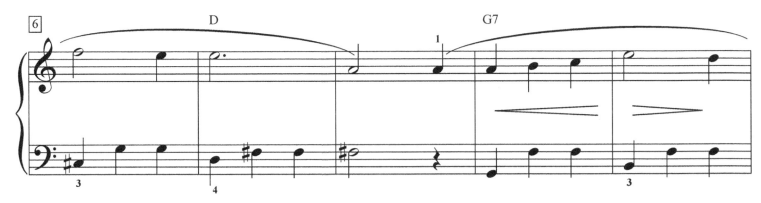

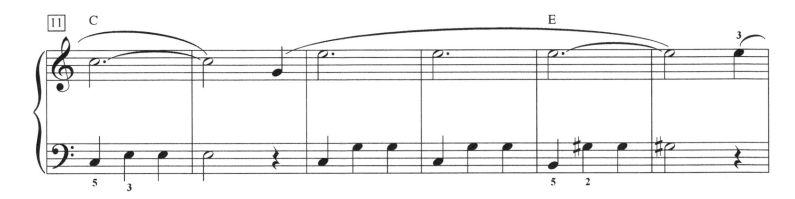

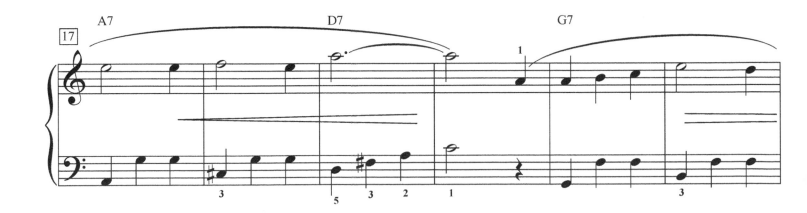

O mio babbino caro

from GIANNI SCHICCHI

By Giacomo Puccini
Arranged by Brenda Dillon

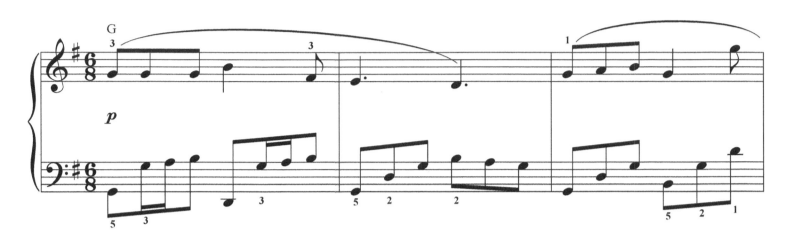

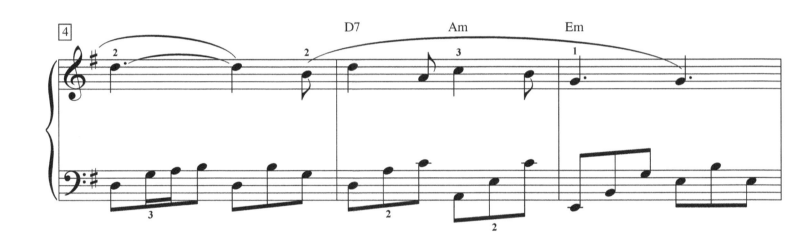

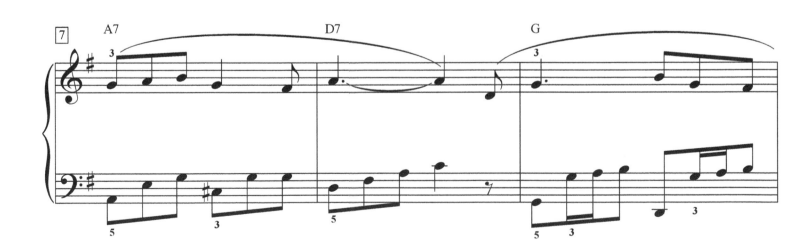

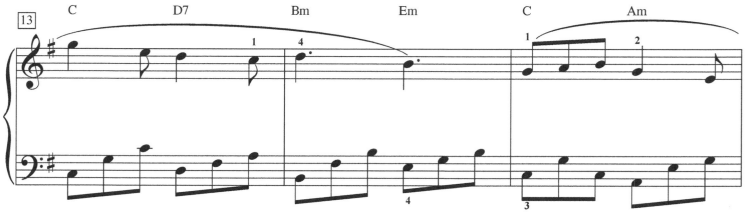

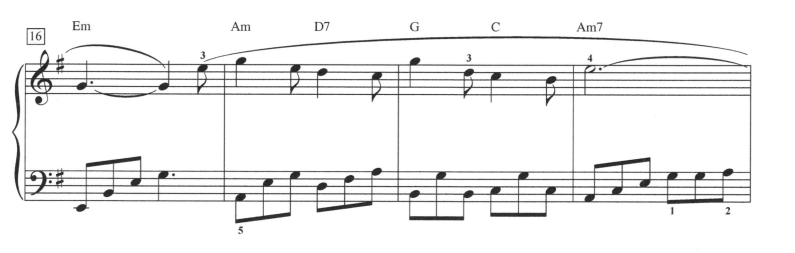

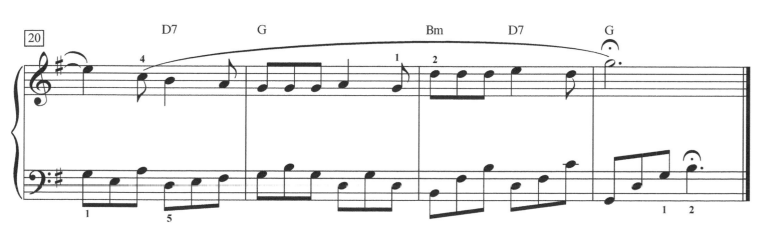

Polovetzian Dance No. 1

from PRINCE IGOR

By Alexander Borodin
Arranged by Brenda Dillon

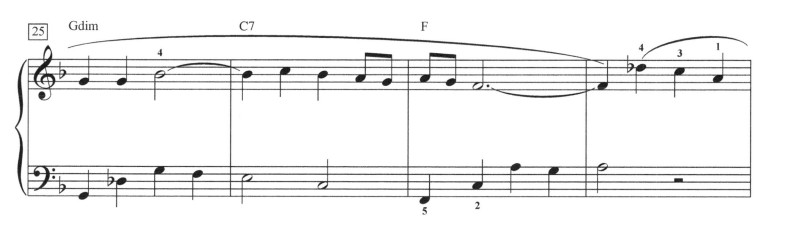

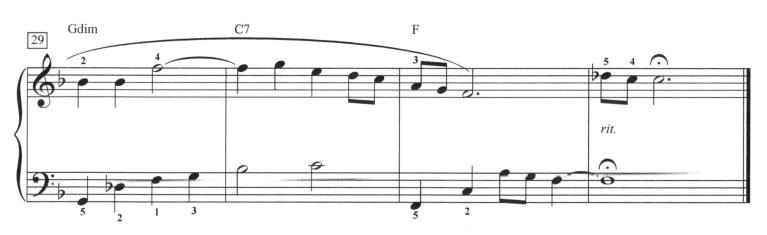

Rhapsody on a Theme of Paganini

Variation XVIII

By Sergei Rachmaninoff
Arranged by Brenda Dillon

Sheep May Safely Graze

By Johann Sebastian Bach
Arranged by Brenda Dillon

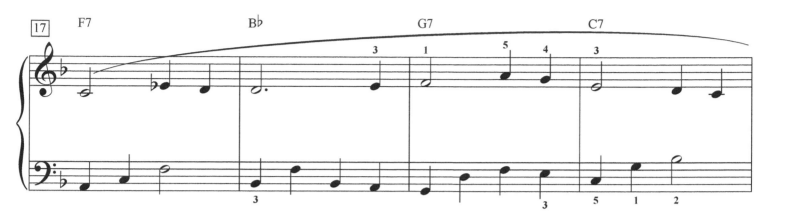

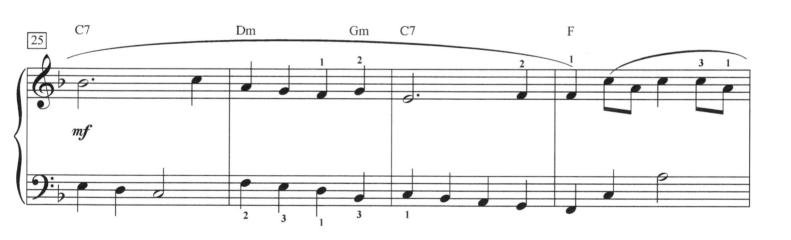

Piano Sonata No. 14 in C# Minor

("Moonlight"), Op. 27, No. 2 First Movement Theme

By Ludwig van Beethoven
Arranged by Brenda Dillon

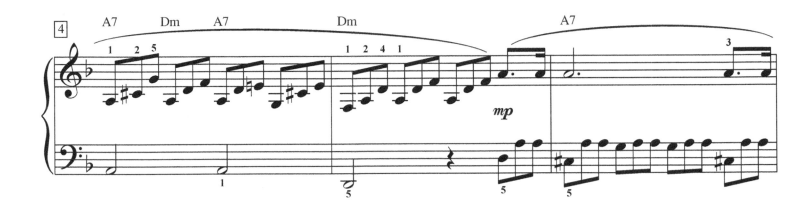

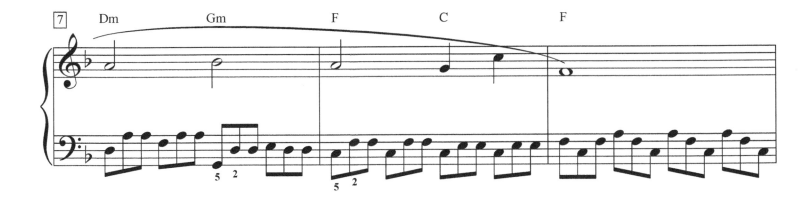

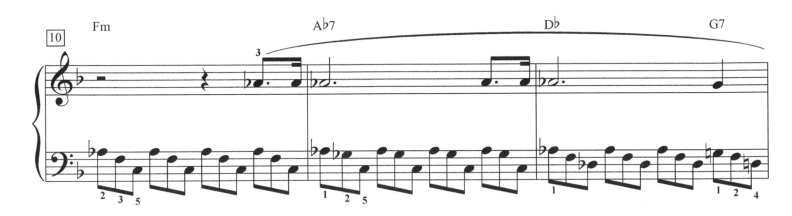

Swan Lake

By Pyotr Ilyich Tchaikovsky
Arranged by Brenda Dillon

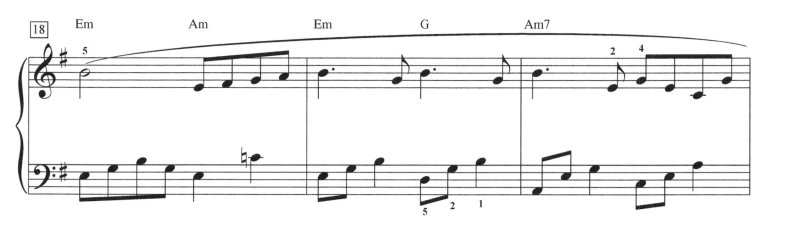

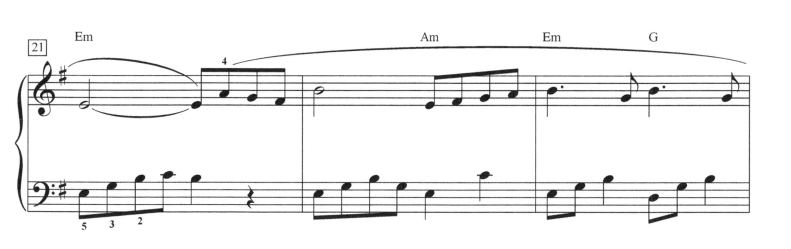

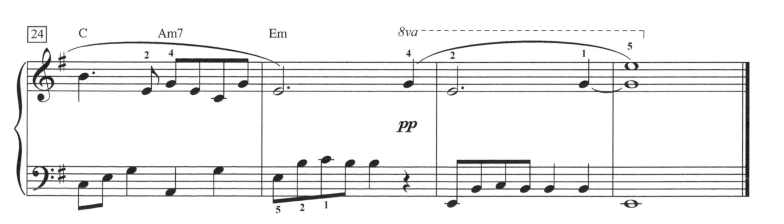

To a Wild Rose

from WOODLAND SKETCHES, OP. 51, NO. 1

By Edward MacDowell
Arranged by Brenda Dillon

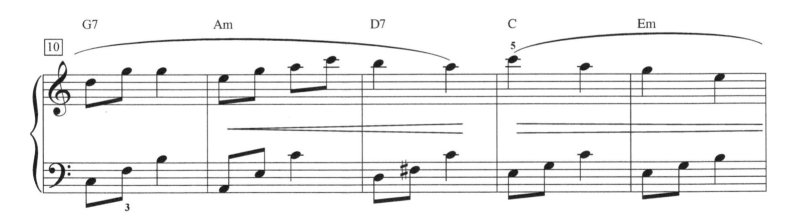

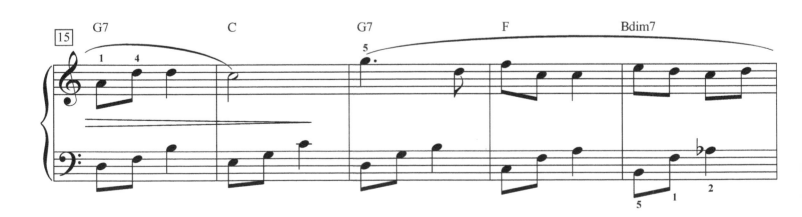

GLOSSARY

Accidentals

Accidentals are sharps (♯), flats (♭) or naturals (♮) added in front of notes.

Dynamics

Crescendo (cresc.)		*Crescendo* means to play gradually louder.
Decrescendo (dim.)		*Decrescendo* and *Diminuendo (dim.)* mean to gradually decrease the dynamic level.
Forte	*f*	*Forte* means to play loudly.
Fortissimo	*ff*	*Fortissimo* means to play very loudly.
Piano	*p*	*Piano* means to play softly.
Pianissimo	*pp*	*Pianissimo* means to play very softly.
Mezzo Forte	*mf*	*Mezzo Forte* means to play moderately loud.
Mezzo Piano	*mp*	*Mezzo Piano* means to play moderately soft.
Subito		*Subito* means an abrupt change in dynamics.

Phrases and Slurs

A phrase is a musical sentence. Slurs often divide music into phrases.

Tempo

♩ = 80

A metronome marking at the beginning of the piece indicates the tempo.

Compositional Variety

Ritard (rit.)		Slow the tempo gradually.
A tempo		Return to the original speed.
Grace note		A small note which is played immediately before the main note and does not add or take away value from that note. The smaller note often has a slash through the stem.
Fermata		A fermata means to hold the note longer than its rhythmic value.
Tie		A tie is a curved line that connects two notes of the same pitch. Hold one sound for the combined value of both notes.
8va/8vb/Loco *8va* - - - - - - ¬		When the sign 8va appears over or under a note or a group of notes, play the note or notes one octave higher than written. 8vb notes are played one octave lower. Loco means to play the notes where they are written.